PARIS TRAVEL GUIDE 2023

<u>Here is everything you need to know about Paris's culture, historical sites, top attractions, cuisines & things to do and see</u>

ALICE D. MORALES

Copyright © 2023 by Alice D. Morales

All rights reserved. No part of this publication may be reproduced, distributed, or transmitted in any form or by any means, including photocopying, recording, or other electronic or mechanical methods, without the prior written permission of the publisher, except in the case of brief quotations embodied in critical reviews and certain other noncommercial uses permitted by copyright law.

Table Of Contents:

INTRODUCTION TO PARIS 5
CHAPTER 1 7
    Interesting Facts About Paris 7
    History Of Paris 11
    Geography And Climate Of Paris 14
    Culture Of The Parisians 18
    The Parisians Disposition To Visitors 22
CHAPTER 2 25
    Essential Things To Know to Prepare Your Visit To Paris 25
    Best Time To Visit Paris 32
    Visa And ID Requirements 43
CHAPTER 3 58
    Transportation In Paris 58
    Best Places To Stay In Paris 63
    Cost Of Food In Paris 74
    Top Paris Attractions To See And Explore 78
    More Top Paris Attractions to See & Explore 94
CHAPTER 4 99
    Basic French Phrases 99
    Staying Safe In Paris 100
    Food To Eat In Paris And Where To Try Them 103
CHAPTER 5 113

Suggested Budget.. 113
24-hours Itinerary.. 114
CONCLUSION.. 118

INTRODUCTION TO PARIS

Anyone who has ever visited Paris, the City of Light, feels romantic. One of the most visited cities in the world is this centuries-old one and for good reason. All types of tourists will find something to do in Paris.

History enthusiasts will be astounded by the depth of a city that has seen two significant revolutions and has been the setting for many of Europe's most powerful kings. The world-famous Louvre museum, the Musee d'Orsay, or any of the many other lesser art museums the city has to offer are perfect places for art enthusiasts to spend a whole lifetime.

The gourmet in you may savor almost every form of gastronomic pleasure since Paris has them all in its quaint cafés, chic restaurants, modest bistros, and delicious patisseries. The greatest department shops and most upscale boutiques in Paris are a fashion lover's paradise.

Two major international airports serve the city of Paris: Charles de Gaulle, often known as Roissy, to the northeast of the city, and Orly to the south. Both airports provide suburban trains (RER), buses, taxis, and metro services to and from the city center.

Administratively, the city of Paris is split into 20 districts, or "Arrondissements," with number 1 starting in the center and extending outward. You can tell which district you are in by looking at the street signs, and the majority of hotels, restaurants and other businesses also provide this information along with the 300+ nearby metro stops.

The Euro was adopted by France, a member of the European Union. Banks and ATMs may be found in abundance in Paris. Additionally, many hotels will exchange money for visitors for the local currency. ATDs are also present at the airports of De Gaulle and Orly.

CHAPTER 1

Interesting Facts About Paris

One of the most well-liked travel destinations in the world is Paris, sometimes referred to as the "City of Lights." It's hardly surprising that Paris has won the hearts of millions of people all over the globe given its magnificent architecture, rich history, and cultural importance. In this paper, we'll look at some of the most remarkable details that make Paris a special and fascinating city.

- A Celtic group known as the Parisii built Paris in the third century BC, more than 2,000 years ago. The architecture and culture of the city still reflect its long and rich past.

- The Eiffel Tower, one of Paris' most recognizable structures, was constructed as a temporary building for the 1889 World's Fair. It was nearly taken apart after the fair since it was only meant to be a temporary building. It was rescued, nonetheless, and has since become an indelible part of the Parisian skyline.

- The Louvre Museum is the biggest in the whole world, with more than 35,000 pieces of art. It is located in Paris. It was first constructed as a stronghold in the 12th century and converted into a museum in 1793.

- Because of its romantic ambiance and cultural importance, Paris is sometimes referred to as the "City of Love." Couples, honeymooners, and anybody else seeking to experience the romance and allure of the city often go there.

- Even though French is the city's official language and a large number of other languages are also spoken there, Paris does not exclusively speak French. The languages you could hear spoken on the streets of Paris include Arabic, Chinese, and English.

- Paris is considered one of the world's fashion capitals, and several renowned fashion brands, like Chanel, Dior, and Yves Saint Laurent, have their headquarters there. An important occasion in the fashion calendar is Paris Fashion Week, which draws designers and admirers from all over the globe.

- Paris is home to several well-known sites, including the Arc de Triomphe, Notre-Dame Cathedral, and the Palace of Versailles, in addition to the Eiffel Tower and the Louvre Museum.

- French food is well-known around the globe, and Paris is no exception. Paris has a long-standing culinary legacy. There are numerous delectable delicacies to sample in Paris, such as baguettes, macarons, and crepes. Additionally, the city is home to a large number of well-known restaurants, including three-star Michelin establishments.

- Famous painters like Picasso, Monet, and Van Gogh were all influenced by Paris, which has long been a source of creative inspiration. The museums and galleries in the city are brimming with the creations of these and other well-known painters.

- The Sorbonne, one of the oldest and most renowned institutions in the world, is located in Paris, which is home to several other notable schools and universities. Since ancient times, students from all over the globe have been drawn to the city because of its reputation for educational brilliance.

With a long and rich history, Paris is a fascinating and distinctive city. Paris is a must-visit location for anybody interested in history, culture, and art because of its well-known monuments, culinary customs, and cultural relevance, among other intriguing facts.

History Of Paris

France's capital city, Paris, has a long and diverse history that dates back more than 2,000 years. Paris has experienced it all, from its modest origins as a little village on the Île de la Cité to becoming one of the most significant cities in the world. We will go through Paris's history in this article and look at the significant figures and events that have influenced this legendary city.

Earlier Years

The Parisii, a Celtic tribe who landed on the Île de la Cité, a tiny island in the middle of the Seine River, are said to have founded Paris in the third century BC. They built a tiny fishing community there and stayed for many years till the region was overrun by the Roman Empire in 52 BC. On the left side of the Seine, the Romans founded Lutetia, a city. Lutetia developed into a significant commercial hub, and its population expanded quickly.

The Medieval Era

For Paris, the Middle Ages were a period of significant transformation. Paris was repeatedly taken over by Viking attacks that started in the ninth century. After the city was reconstructed, work on the Notre Dame Cathedral started in the 12th century. It is one of Paris' most recognizable structures and took more than 200 years to finish. King Louis IX erected the Sainte-Chapelle, a beautiful Gothic chapel, in the 13th century to contain sacred artifacts.

Enlightenment and Renaissance

Paris saw significant development throughout the Renaissance and Enlightenment eras. King Francis I., attracted Italian artists and architects to Paris in the 16th century, and the city soon established itself as a hub for culture and the arts. The 16th century saw the start of the Louvre Museum's long-term building. It was once a fortification, then it became a royal residence, and last it became a museum.

The French Revolution started in the 18th century, and Paris was crucial to the subsequent events. The French Revolution began on July 14, 1789, with the storming of the Bastille, and the Reign of Terror that followed witnessed the execution of hundreds of people.

Modern Era

Paris had significant expansion and change over the 19th and 20th centuries. Napoleon III started a large reconstruction effort in the 19th century that included erecting the well-known Eiffel Tower.

Additionally, Paris developed into a hub of fashion and culture, and notable authors and painters like Ernest Hemingway and Pablo Picasso made the city their home. Paris was invaded by German soldiers during World War II in the 20th century, and the city suffered immensely. In the post-war period, it was renovated and turned into a hub of political and artistic activity.

Paris is a thriving city today with a fascinating past and vibrant culture. Millions of people visit its sites and museums each year, and it is still a significant hub for fashion, art, and literature. Events and individuals from Paris's history have formed the city, and it will continue to change and expand in the years to come.

Geography And Climate Of Paris

The country's north-central region is home to Paris, the capital of France. It is 105.4 square kilometers in size and is located along the Seine River. The city is one of the most well-liked tourist destinations in the globe due to its scenic boulevards, ancient buildings, and well-known attractions. We shall examine Paris's topography, climate, and its effects on the history and culture of the city in this article.

Geography of Paris

The Île-de-France region, which is where Paris is situated, is the most populous area in France. The Seine River, which runs through the city from east to west, bends about where it is located. The city is situated on the Île de la Cité and the Île Saint-Louis, two large islands, and is encircled by several hills, notably Montmartre and Belleville. The Seine River, which was instrumental in the growth of the city, affected the geography of the area.

Throughout history, the Seine River has been crucial for the movement of both commodities and people. Since ancient times, trade routes have crossed the navigable river's banks. Today, the Seine River is a well-liked tourist destination where people can go on boat trips and see the city's iconic sites from the water.

Climate of Paris

The climate of Paris is temperate and oceanic, with pleasant winters and chilly summers. With an average temperature ranging from 5°C in January to 20°C in July, the city has four different seasons. Additionally, the city receives some rainfall throughout the year, with May and June being the wettest.

The culture and way of life of Paris have been shaped by its climate. Outdoor sports have become a common activity for Parisians because of the city's numerous parks and gardens and the pleasant temperature. The city's famous sidewalk cafés, a symbol of Parisian culture, are also a result of the climate there. Parisians like sitting outdoors in the summer, drinking wine or coffee while taking in the beautiful weather and their friends' companionship.

The climate of the city is also influenced by the Seine River. The city is kept warmer in the winter and cooler in the summer because of the river's ability to regulate the temperature. The city's humidity is also influenced by the river, which may make the summers seem humid when they aren't.

Paris's Environmental Problems

Paris, despite its attractive exterior, confronts some environmental issues. High levels of air pollution brought on by industrial activities and increased traffic have recently raised concerns about the city's air quality. The establishment of bike lanes, pedestrian zones, and expanded public transit are just a few of the actions the city has taken to solve this problem.

The difficulty of trash management exists in Paris as well. The city generates a large quantity of the garbage, and its landfills are almost full. The city has established steps to limit trash output, such as a ban on single-use plastics, and recycling programs to address this problem.

Conclusion

In conclusion, the topography and climate of Paris have greatly influenced the development of the history and culture of the city. The design and growth of the city have been impacted by the Seine River, which has also been an important transit route. Parisians enjoy outdoor activities and sidewalk cafés because of the city's warm temperature. But to maintain its prosperity and sustainability, the city must also handle environmental issues like garbage management and air pollution.

Culture Of The Parisians

Paris is renowned for both its illustrious cultural history and its affluent way of life. The inhabitants of Paris, known as Parisians, have a distinctive culture that is reflected in the history, art, fashion, and gastronomy of the city. We shall examine the distinctive aspects of Parisian culture in this article.

Art and Literature

For ages, Paris has been a center for the arts and literature. The city is home to some of the most well-known museums, art galleries, and literary cafés in the world. Parisians are renowned for their appreciation of the arts and literature, and prominent authors and painters have lived there throughout history.

There are several renowned museums in Paris, including the Louvre, which is home to some of the most well-known pieces of art in the whole world, such as the Mona Lisa. Smaller art galleries and shows are also popular among Parisians to attend.

Parisian culture also places a strong emphasis on literature. Numerous well-known authors have called the city home, including Ernest Hemingway, F. Scott Fitzgerald, and Victor Hugo. Parisians have a long history of reading, and the city is filled with literary cafés and booksellers.

Style and Fashion

Paris is renowned for its fashion and style, and the people of Paris are renowned for their affluent sense of style. Numerous renowned fashion brands, like Chanel, Dior, and Yves Saint Laurent, have their headquarters in the city.

Parisians are renowned for their subtle elegance and minimalist style of dressing. Parisians get inspiration from the city's many fashion bloggers and influencers for their street style, which is another attribute of the city.

Food and Drink

The love of fine cuisine and beverages is well-known among Parisians. Numerous renowned eateries may be found in the city, notably the three-Michelin-starred Alain Ducasse in the Plaza Athénée.

The city's many cafés and brasseries, where people may eat classic French fare like croissants, escargot, and steak frites, are also popular among Parisians. Parisians like sipping on a glass of red or white wine with their meals since the city is also well-known for its wine.

Socializing

The love of socializing and spending time with friends and family is well-known among Parisians. Parisians like to get together for a cup of coffee or a bottle of wine at the city's cafes and bars.

Parisians are renowned for their enthusiasm for cultural events including musical performances, art exhibits, and theatrical productions. Parisians like going to these events with their friends and family since the city provides many cultural events all year round.

The rich and diversified culture of Parisians reflects the long history and rich cultural legacy of the city. Parisians enjoy interacting with their friends and loved ones and are renowned for their appreciation of the arts, literature, fashion, and gastronomy. Cafes, museums, and cultural events all play a significant role in Parisian culture and add to the city's distinct attractiveness.

The Parisians Disposition To Visitors

The inclination of Parisians toward guests is one of their distinctive personality qualities. Although some would argue that Parisians are unwelcoming to visitors, this is not always the case. Parisians' attitudes regarding tourists are varied, and they may change depending on the circumstance.

Generally speaking, Parisians value tourists who respect the city and its way of life. Parisians are inclined to welcome visitors who make an effort to learn French, observe local traditions, and enjoy the beauty of the city. Visitors that are obnoxious, inconsiderate, or boisterous won't likely get a warm welcome.

Parisians are renowned for their love of mingling and discussion as well. Parisians are inclined to welcome visitors who are prepared to engage in discussion. Parisians take pleasure in expressing their views on a variety of subjects, including politics, culture, and the arts.

Despite this, Parisians might be wary of outsiders. This is more often a result of a cultural gap than necessarily being unfriendly. Parisians may not be as outgoing with strangers as those from other cultures because they respect their privacy.

It's also important to keep in mind that Parisians often lead hectic lifestyles. This is particularly true in tourist-heavy locations where Parisians may be under stress from negotiating congested streets and public transportation. In these circumstances, Parisians may come to seem distant or uninterested to tourists, although this does not always represent how they feel about them.

In general, showing respect for the city and its culture, being open to dialogue, and being aware that Parisians could have a different approach to socializing and engaging with strangers is crucial to getting along with the populace. Visitors may connect well with Parisians and obtain a better understanding of the city's distinctive culture and personality by adopting the correct mindset and approach.

CHAPTER 2

Essential Things To Know to Prepare Your Visit To Paris

For good reason, Paris is a popular fantasy vacation spot. It is the birthplace of avant-garde design and art, gourmet food, and architecture rich in glitz and history. You may finally visit the City of Lights this year as France is officially welcoming tourists!

However, Paris offers more than just romance, fine wine, and creative endeavors. Additionally, given the language barrier, it may be difficult for visitors to find their way about the European city. As a result, we have provided the finest advice for visiting Paris, including the best seasons to go to and how to avoid scams.

1. Paris is more than simply a city for lovers

The typical first-time traveler's perception of Paris is romantic candlelight meals in an art nouveau café, the sun setting behind the Eiffel Tower, and French folks waxing poetic about life and love. This is not to imply that they do not apply to Paris. However, if you're a gourmet, make sure your schedule includes Michelin-starred eateries and well-known neighborhood cafés. If you're a history enthusiast, this book will more than likely pique your interest. Therefore, you can be sure that Paris has intriguing things to do, no matter what your interests may be.

2. Go when it's not as busy.

The off-peak months of April and October are without a doubt the ideal times to visit Paris. fewer tourists, lower hotel prices, and a beautiful natural spectacle right in the city. While fans of pumpkin spice lattes will appreciate strolls through parks and streets lined with foliage, spring lovers will like the pink colors of cherry blossoms. Professional picture sessions, such as weddings, family portraits, and engagements, both make for the ideal settings.

3. Reserve lodging close to the action.

In Paris, you may choose a hotel from one of the 20 arrondissements, or districts. There are many museums and tourist sites in each of these areas that might aid in your decision. The 18th contains Montmartre, the 3rd and 4th share Le Marais, and the 5th is known as the city's Latin Quarter. Plan since lodgings here might be more expensive.

4. Invest in a Paris Pass

Using the Paris travel pass, a lady is seen touring Paris
The next step is to decide what to do now that you are aware of the best time to go and where to stay. Thank goodness for the Paris Pass, a versatile multipass that is affordable and ideal for first-timers. Enjoy skip-the-line access for the duration of your ticket and visit more than 75

sites and museums across the city for up to 4 days. To aid you in navigating Paris a little bit better, you'll also get a guidebook and a free metrocard.

5. Put on comfy shoes

Paris's cobblestone streets may be attractive to the eye, but they are deadly for first-time tourists. Wear your most comfortable pair of shoes or sandals for the time being since walking is the greatest way to experience the city. Ditch the heels. You should also consider certain sights' great distances, such as the fact that the Eiffel Tower is on the other side of Notre Dame. Even days after your journey, bodily pains are a given while traveling back and forth between locations.

6. Make use of transit

In addition to walking, using the metro and renting a Velib are excellent ways to see Paris. However, how precisely do you utilize them?

You just need to purchase a Paris Pass or a Paris Metro Pass to use the metro. Both tickets provide unrestricted use of the Paris Metro system, enabling visitors to explore any part of the city. A public bike-sharing program called Velib, meanwhile, has more than 1,800 stations spread out around the city. Either a normal bike or an e-bike may be rented for a certain period, then returned to a station close by before the rental period is over. To travel across France comfortably and without fuss, you may also use the train.

7. Be wary of frauds and pickpockets

You should be on the lookout for fraudsters and pickpockets since you'll be using the subway. Make careful to leave big sums of cash and valuables like your passport at your hotel since tourists are walking targets. There are a number of these folks you may encounter at tourist destinations, some of whom will urge you politely to join environmental petitions or wear friendship bracelets with them. If you can, try to stay away from these situations, and if you do find yourself in one, get out as soon as possible.

8. Work on fundamental French words

Despite being very hard to learn, French is a lovely language. You should learn a few additional words while you're at it as it's traditional to say "Bonjour" to store employees and service personnel before placing an order or making a purchase. Here are a few examples you may find helpful:

Merci (Thank you), Pardon (Sorry), Comment allez-vous? (What's your name?), D'accord (Okay), Excusez-moi (Excuse me), and Où se trouve la station de métro la plus proche? (Where is the closest metro station?).

9. Remember to include a travel adapter

Despite how clear it may seem, few people are aware that power connectors in Paris are different from those found elsewhere. European power plugs have two prongs, and their sockets are deep and round. Budget lodgings and bed-and-breakfasts most likely won't be able to provide this luxury, although upscale hotels may have additional power outlets in their rooms. Before you forget it again, put a travel adapter on your list of travel essentials.

10. Make reservations in advance at restaurants

Everywhere you travel in France, fine eating is a must-try experience. However, given the abundance of Michelin-starred restaurants in Paris, the issue could be a little more difficult. If you don't want to wait in line for meals after you've decided where to dine, be sure to make a reservation in advance. You just must try the chef's table at Marsan par Hélène Darroze, the Comté cheese soufflé at PavIllon, and the choux pastry Paris Brest at Le Serva, to name a few of our faves. n.

11. Always verify closing times

Parisians enjoy leisure and take their time, much like people in most of Europe's capitals. The majority of stores and restaurants shut on Sundays, supper doesn't start until 7:30 p.m., and enterprises take summer vacations in August. Opening hours may fluctuate throughout the year due to seasonal changes and daylight savings time, mostly. You, busybodies, may not understand these schedule modifications, but while in Paris, follow the local customs. Make it a practice to verify a location's opening hours at least two days in advance.

Best Time To Visit Paris

All year long, there is enough to do on the streets of Paris. Therefore, it stands to reason that any time is the ideal moment to visit Paris. There is a lot to discover and enjoy in Paris, from street performances and wine tasting to entertaining events and food carnivals. Your trip to Paris will be memorable since each of the city's four different seasons has something unique and endearing to offer.

Everyone will encourage you to visit Paris if it's your first trip in the spring when the weather is at its finest. You may enjoy strolling around the Parisian streets and taking in the city like the inhabitants do since the sun is warm and brilliant, the days are long, and the weather is pleasant. The city is busiest during this time of year, costs are higher, and you may not be able to take it all in at your leisure.

You can discover another season that suits your preferences better depending on your hobbies. Yes, each season has advantages and disadvantages, and we'll help you choose the ideal time of year to visit Paris in this post.

Paris often has warm weather year-round. The winters never dip below freezing, and the summers never become too hot. The most enjoyable season is spring, which lasts from

March to May. Summer, which lasts from June to August, comes next. October through November is considered autumn, and at that time it begins to grow chilly and rainy, although the weather is still pleasant and has its charm. Paris's winters are not very chilly. Although it never gets below freezing in December, January, or February, it still seems chilly due to the low humidity levels.

Everyone should go to Paris at least once since it is such a beautiful place. There is a lot to do and see in this area, whether you are traveling alone, with friends, or with your family.

Peak Season (March-August)

The ideal seasons to visit Paris are spring and summer. There are several events that the city holds to spread happiness, and the weather is ideal for sightseeing. These six months are perfect for travel if you want to see Paris as the locals do.

Shoulder Season (September-November)

Although there is a small chill in the air and there is a larger chance of rain, everyone is still welcome in the city. This is an excellent time to visit Paris since the crowds are starting to thin out.

Low Season (December-February)

Parisian winters are chilly and rainy. However, when it snows, the city has an ethereal beauty. The city is seldom affected by frost, and most snow melts within a day or two. Every traveler's fantasy is to experience the romance of Christmas in Paris, and you can easily do so by organizing a winter vacation here.

Paris in Spring (March - May)
Temperature: Avg. of 19 degrees high to 04 degrees low

The weather in Paris in the spring is unpredictable. While it is often warm throughout the day, the weather varies gently during the day and becomes colder as the evening draws near. It starts to grow warmer as we approach May. Although there is often rain, it seldom lasts long since the streets immediately dry out. The days are lovely and lengthy, and you get to be outside more. Unquestionably, this is the most ideal time of year to visit Paris.

Important occurrences: Now is the season for outdoor sports. In the third week of May, if you happen to be in Paris, you may watch the French Open. However, the Paris Marathon, where thousands of people run more than 26 kilometers, is first on the city's agenda. The weather is perfect for outdoor picnics right now, and you can set up shop in any of the city's numerous gardens. The Foire du Trône, a funfair of exceptional size and maybe the oldest as well, is the centerpiece of this season. Everyone will remain captivated by the rides, food, music, and fireworks.

Reasons to go right away: This time of year, Paris is stunning. Your vacation will be fantastic thanks to the combination of the weather, the celebrations, and the people.

Know before you go: This is one of the busiest seasons to visit Paris, so be prepared for sky-high prices wherever you go. Order in advance to avoid disappointment.

Be prepared to change your plans at a moment's notice and always carry rain gear.

Paris in Summer (June - August)
Temperature: Avg. of 24 degrees high to 13 degrees low

Paris in the summer is described as being comfortably pleasant and welcoming due to the weather. Since the days are long and bright, you may stroll around the city while taking in all the attractions. Since exams are over and people are out on the streets with their families and children, there is a festive atmosphere everywhere. Summer thunderstorms are to be expected, thus we advise you to prepare accordingly for the summer weather in Paris.

Events of note: The Tropical Carnival of Paris ushers in summer in Paris. It almost seems as if the whole city has been waiting for this moment to go to the streets and take in the floats, costumes, and the full shebang. Music enthusiasts may unwind and indulge their senses at the socially conscious Solidays and We Love Green events, as well as Fête de la Musique, which is observed as Music Day in Paris. At the La Villette Outdoor Movie Theatre, movie lovers may see carefully chosen films.

Why you should go now: Due to the good weather and the festivities, this is one of the most well-liked periods to visit Paris. Nowhere else can you spend the summer as leisurely as in Paris.

The city is congested in the summer, so be aware before you go. In these months, children, teenagers, families, and visitors all go to Paris's landmarks and tourist attractions. Both the waiting times and the cost of the tickets have increased.

Reminder: Paris is mostly not air-conditioned. As a result, when it becomes heated, it might be uncomfortable. Ensure that your lodging has air conditioning so you may unwind comfortably.

Paris in Autumn (September to November)
Temperature: Avg. of 21 degrees high to 05 degrees low

Climate: With the onset of fall, you may bid farewell to the summer's humidity. Less heat and fewer people are present. Although the days are beginning to become shorter, the Parisian fall weather is still ideal for touring. Even though it's still raining, the days are chilly and the evenings are growing progressively cooler as October approaches. Paris is a lovely city in the fall, and you can take some incredible photographs of renowned landmarks with the tree's autumnal hues.

Important developments: Paris gives away many of its monuments for free. During European Heritage Days, you may visit numerous monuments, even some that are often closed. La Parisienne is a race that is mostly raced by women to raise money for breast cancer research. You may wish to take part in it (even if it's only on the sidelines). You may experience art as you've never experienced it before in October by attending the Nuit Blanche all night long (All-nighter). You may see this exhibition of artwork by local artists for free. It is shown across the city. The Beaujolais Nouveau is where you can sample the fresh wines of the year if you're in Paris in November.

Why you should go right now: The crowds are beginning to thin out, and you may have the city mostly to yourself. But not much yet, the temperature is dropping.

Before traveling, be aware that hotel costs have not yet decreased even though this is not the busiest travel period. To obtain lodging at an affordable price, significant study is required.

Advice: Always carry a jacket. There is a cold in the air even though it is bright.

Paris in Winter (December to February)
Temperature: Avg. of 8 degrees high to 02 degrees low

Weather: Winter has officially arrived, and even the trees are starting to lose most of their leaves. The days and nights are both frigid as the sun is about to go on its yearly vacation. The winter weather in Paris does not diminish the city's attractiveness, which is still breathtaking even when it is covered in a light layer of snow. The days are rather brief since the sun sets every day at 5 o'clock.

Significant occurrences in Paris in the winter are stunning. Spending hours browsing the inviting window displays of renowned department shops like Printemps and Galeries Lafayette may be done while strolling around Paris' streets. Try your go at ice skating at one of the many temporary rinks that have been put up across the city. On the first level of the Eiffel, you can even ice skate.

How about it as a trip wish list? Several Christmas markets appear, and you may just observe people walking by engaged in their shopping while sipping warm wine or drinking hot chocolate. Paris' Fashion Week takes place in January. Receive early access to what the fashion industry has in store for the rest of us.

Why you should go now: Paris is lovely in the winter because fewer people are there, so you can enjoy the greatest vistas and spend the least amount of time at each sight.

It's important to prepare ahead and cram as much sightseeing as possible into the few daylight hours when you go.

Though chilly, it is magnificent. Bring a heavy jacket and plenty of warm clothing.

Visa And ID Requirements

Depending on your nationality, you may need to first get a visa for France if you want to go there for a shorter amount of time than 90 days.

You are only allowed to remain in France for a maximum of 90 days within a 180-day term with a tourist visa. In general, you are allowed to travel with this visa to the other Schengen nations throughout that time, except in situations where it is designated as a visa with limited territorial validity.

1. Who is eligible for a France tourist visa?

It all depends on your nationality whether you need or do not require a short-stay visa to visit European France or its overseas territories, collectivities, departments, and regions.

Any sort of visa is not required for entry into or stay in France if you are a citizen of Andorra, Monaco, Switzerland, or any other member of the European Union or the European Economic Area.

If you are a citizen of one of these nations, you will also not need to apply for a tourist visa to France. If you need a visa to enter France, you need one to enter Monaco as well.

If you are not a citizen of one of the nations mentioned or listed above, you will likely need to apply for a visa before being granted entry to France.

2. Things to Think About Before Obtaining a French Tourist Visa

Before requesting a French tourist visa, you should:

- Look at your passport. Verify that the required length of validity is met by your passport. If not, ask for a fresh one before requesting a visa.
- Plan your trip ahead of time. After you have finished everything else, do not put it off until the evening before your visa appointment. It's possible that you won't be able to board a flight on the specified day.
- Ensure that everything is in working order. Instead of thinking, "Maybe they won't notice this," or "They can't make a big deal out of such a minor thing," stop yourself. You should follow all protocols and fulfill all standards since consular agents will carefully review everything.

3. When Can I Send in My Application?

Submitting the application file at the right time is crucial for a positive outcome on your France Tourist Visa application. According to the France tourist visa rules the earliest that you can make the application is six months before your booked flight to France.

The latest you may do it, however, is two weeks before the date of your scheduled travel.

4. In which location should I send my application for a tourist visa to France?

You may need to submit your application at the following locations, depending on the French authorities' regulations for visa entry in your country of residence:

- the French embassy's consular division in your nation.
- a representation of France in your nation.
- a third-party visa processing facility that France has contracted with to handle visa applications in your nation.

- French authorities in your country of residency have outsourced the filing of visas to a French embassy, consulate, or visa processing facility in a nearby country.

What if I need to visit countries other than France?

You may need to apply at a different embassy rather than in France if you plan on visiting the Schengen Area to visit countries other than France. For some people, this could seem a little difficult, but it's rather easy.

In the beginning, make a list of the nations you want to visit together with the number of days you anticipate staying in each. The embassy where you intend to spend most of your time is where you should apply. You must apply at the embassy of the nation where you will spend more days, in this example the Embassy of France, if you are traveling to Germany and

France and will be there for three days in the first and five in the latter.

On the other hand, if you want to spend an equal number of days in two or more countries—for example, two in France, two in Germany, and two in Switzerland—you must apply at the embassy of the nation where you will be arriving first.

5. How Can I Get a French Tourist Visa?

Particularly for those who have never needed to get a visa before, the application procedure for a French tourist visa may appear challenging and tedious. However, if you write out the actions you need to do and take them methodically, you will be able to accomplish your objective and get the visa:

- Complete the French Tourist Schengen visa application form.
- Gather the necessary paperwork

- Schedule a meeting
- Pay the charges.
- Show up When the appointment is made

Complete the French Tourist Schengen visa application form

The France Embassy on your country's website has the application for a tourist visa there. If you don't, you may request that the embassy send you a form by email online.

Fill out the application form truthfully and accurately. Remember that the information you provide in this form must match that in the other papers, otherwise your application will likely be denied. Please remember to print it twice and to sign both versions at the end.

Gather the necessary paperwork

Gather the necessary paperwork for a France tourist visa after applying. Make sure you have copies and originals of every document. On the day of your appointment, be sure to bring all required paperwork; otherwise, your application may be rejected.

To apply for a tourist visa to France, you must provide the following paperwork:

- application for a French tourist visa completed. Make sure you fill out the proper form and that the data you provide is accurate.
- two pictures that would be used for a passport. Their age cannot exceed three months.
- your passport is current. It must be current—issued within the past ten years—and valid for at least three months after the conclusion of your intended stay in France. The passport must have at least two vacant pages before the visa sticker may be applied.
- replicas of earlier visas. Copy of all visas you have ever had, for any place in the globe.

- Your stay in France and the Schengen Area will be covered by travel medical insurance to the tune of at least €30,000.
- Certificate of criminal history from the candidate's native country attesting to their lack of participation in any active investigations
- evidence that the visa cost has been paid.
- Itinerary for travel. This document details your activities while you are in France, and your arrival and departure dates, and it also provides evidence of pre-arranged transportation, such as the purchase of airline tickets.
- Proof of Housing in France. It might be a hotel or hostel reservation or a letter of invitation if you want to stay with friends or family.
- means of support. Proof that, if you choose to, you have the financial resources to fund the whole of your stay in France and the other Schengen nations. This might be a bank statement that is no more than three days old and covers the

previous three months, or it could be a scholarship certificate that details the amount you will get throughout your whole stay.

Schedule a meeting

For your meeting with a consular representative of the French embassy, you must make an appointment. Every candidate above the age of 12 must attend the interview. On the website of the French embassy or consulate in your country, make an online appointment for the interview. You will need to visit the embassy to make an appointment if that option is not available in your nation.

Pay the charges.

On the day of your appointment, at the embassy, consulate, or visa application facility, you must pay the visa fee before going to the interview. The cost of a tourist visa for France is €80.

The payment must be made in euros or the local currency, depending on the embassy's exchange rates.

Show up When the appointment is made

Attend your appointment at the France embassy, consulate, or visa application office on time. Your appointment can be canceled if you arrive late; in that case, you will need to make another appointment and wait your turn.

Wear something that feels good on you and has a somewhat more formal appearance. Don't worry about it. To avoid having a mess on your hands during the appointment with the consular official, organize your paperwork before the meeting. Your vacation to France, the reason for your visit, and other topics will be covered by the interviewer. This interview usually lasts no more than ten minutes.

6. Validity of France Tourist Visa

The French embassy that granted you the visa determines how long it is valid. A French tourist visa may be valid for a maximum of three months and six months.

At the present, the embassy could grant you a visa for the necessary time frame, such as ten days, three weeks, or even three or five days. However, you may still get multiple entries, and a three-month valid visa, especially if you often visit the Schengen region.

8. Can I go to other nations in Europe?

Depending on the kind of Schengen visa you are issued. When a visa becomes valid, you may travel across the whole Schengen region if the visa sticker in your passport reads "The Schengen States" or "États Schengen" or similar phrases in another EU language.

On the other hand, if your visa specifies "Schengen states (-the acronym of a nation)" it implies you cannot visit only that country, while "Schengen states (-ES)" suggests you may travel to all of the Schengen states except for Spain. You may also get a visa that merely says the abbreviations of the countries you're allowed to visit, such as "F, FIN, GR," which implies you can only go to France, Finland, and Greece.

9. Hints for traveling with a tourist visa to France

You could have traveled before, or at least, you've taken a tourist trip to France. However, a few more pointers could be very beneficial for you. Following the receipt of your France tourist visa:

- List the French locations that you wish to visit. All visitors visiting France on a tourist visa naturally want to see the Eiffel Tower, the Louvre, and the Arch of Triumph. You should be aware, however,

that getting from one location to another will take time. So, instead of merely traveling from the Eiffel Tower to the Arch of Triumph, spend some time seeing the locations in between. That, my friend, is what you call wise travel preparation.
- Adapt your clothing to the weather. The weather in France should guide your packing decisions. Always pack at least two outfits—one for warmer days than anticipated and another for cooler weather.
- Bring some relaxed sneakers. There's a chance you'll have to walk a lot.

Using a tourist visa while in France:

- cash in hand. The majority of the time, you can pay with a card, but sometimes, especially in smaller stores and restaurants, you may need to pay with cash.
- Pickpocketing should be avoided. particularly in busy areas like museums and heavily trafficked streets. They can

sneak up on you from behind or take your wallet or phone from your hands. Keep these items nearby at all times.
- Examine the cuisine available on the streets. You should at least try one of them, whether it's a baguette sandwich, grilled cheese, or crêpes. Without experiencing the local cuisine, a trip to France is nothing.

CHAPTER 3

Transportation In Paris

Metro

The quickest, cheapest, and most convenient method to get across Paris is via Métro. The entrance is denoted by a giant yellow letter "M," and there are over 300 metro stations and 16 different metro lines.

Metros operate every day, including on public holidays, from roughly 6 am until around 12.45 am or 1.45 am (from Sunday through Thursday) (on Friday and Saturday).

Metros operate at varying intervals depending on the time of day: During rush hour, metros run every two minutes.

Where can I purchase a metro ticket?

One metro ticket costs €1.90; ten tickets cost €18.60 (ask for "un carnet"). At automated ticket vending machines in metro stations, in cig shops, and online.

RER (suburban express railway)

There are 5 lines of the RER rail system that service Paris and the surrounding area (Ile-de-France). On RATP and SNCF signage and maps, each line's characteristic color is shown.

RER trains operate every day, including on public holidays, from roughly 6 am until around 12.45 am.

Except for passing your ticket through the automated gates again on your way out, the RER functions in Paris in a manner that is almost identical to that of the metro. The same ticket may be used for the whole trip if your RER station has a link to the metro.

Transilien (regional train)

Transiliens are regional trains that leave from busy Parisian railway stations (Nord, Est, Lyon, Austerlitz, Montparnasse, Saint-Lazare). In railway stations, metro/RER stations, and at "Ile-de-France" ticket counters and automatic ticket machines, tickets and passes may be purchased. At the ticket counters at railway stations, free schedule pamphlets are offered. Commuter lines are a supplement to the RER network and link to it often.

Tramway

T1, T2, T3, and T4 are the four tram lines that serve Paris's outskirts.

Tickets for the tram are the same as those for the RER and the metro in Paris.

Bus

Panthéon by city bus Daniel Thierry is an OTCP. Buses go through the city's center, along the Seine's banks, and through historic neighborhoods on several different bus routes.

The metro network is complemented by 64 bus routes that run alongside it. Travel times have been shortened by the addition of designated bus lanes on major thoroughfares. Allow 5 minutes for every stop, or sometimes longer if traffic is heavy, to get an estimate of how long your trip will take.

Buses run Monday through Saturday from 7 am until 12:30 pm. At 8.30 p.m., some lines stop service. On Sundays and public holidays, over half of the bus routes are open.

On the front, above the driver's cabin, and on the sides of the bus, there are indications of the line number and direction. To signal the bus driver to stop, extend your hand at the bus stop.

The amount of time before the next bus will come is shown on electronic display signs at bus stops. Additionally, USB outlets for charging your smartphone are sometimes available at bus stops.

Glass shelters or plain poles are both used as bus stops. Both a map of the bus routes taken and the number of the bus lines that serve the stop are shown. Additionally, they provide the first and latest bus arrival times as well as the typical bus frequency for that stop.

You board the bus in the front and exit at the rear, center, or middle of the vehicle. You may board and exit an articulated bus via any of its doors; just press the button next to each door to unlock it. To authenticate your pass or punch your ticket, remember to. When the bus is moving, push one of the red buttons inside to ask for a stop. A "stop requested" light is shown in front of the driver's compartment.

Noctilien

A late-night Paris bus The Thinkstock
From 12.30 a.m. to 5.30 a.m., Paris and the surrounding area are served by the Noctilien night bus service. Everyone may use public transportation since 47 lines run across Paris and the surrounding area.

You may use a trip pass or a metro/bus ticket as long as they are valid for the relevant zones (the same zones as for the metro/RER).

Best Places To Stay In Paris

Paris is a large city, without intending to express the obvious. large. A place to stay in Paris That may be the million-euro question, but that may be overreacting a bit given that we're going to break down the nicest areas of the city to your advantage. In Paris, every choice seems to be worthwhile, but it is evident that certain areas are superior to others in terms of dining, nightlife, shopping, history, and other factors.

The greatest locations to stay in Paris are located in a collection of municipalities that are part of a very large metropolis (did we mention that?).

There is always a new area to discover, accommodations to book, and restaurants to try, so it doesn't matter whether you're a Paris veteran or know your way around the city like the back of your hand. Consider this your indispensable guide to daily living in Paris (believe us, we're the pros). You'll be planning a second vacation before this one is through since there is so much to see and do. Once again,

1. Saint-Germain-des-Prés.

Saint-Germain-des-Prés is the only place to go for a five-star Parisian experience. This is where the major 20th-century cultural movements in Paris flourished, where Godard and Giacometti shared cafés and bookstores with Sartre and de Beauvoir. In the many small shops and boutiques, that era still exists, and

Saint-Germain is hard to top for genuine café culture.

When night comes, the Latin Quarter surrounding the Sorbonne is where you'll discover bustling, student-packed pubs, restaurants, and clubs. By day, relax amid the lakes and palm trees of the adjoining Jardin du Luxembourg. In Saint-Germain, high-end retailers like Cartier and Sonia Rykiel have stores. Restaurants might be hit or miss, so stick with vulnerable establishments like the oldest restaurant in Paris, Le Procope, or Fish La Boissonnerie for the best seafood.

2. South Pigalle

South Pigalle, sometimes known as "So-Pi " locally, is to Paris what Peckham or Dalston is to London: very fashionable. The hottest nightlife trends, including fusion bistros (Buvette), concept hotels (Le Pigalle), and secret cocktail bars (Lulu White's), can all be found here, just below Pigalle's sex stories and the Moulin

Rouge. The Rue des Martyrs is a foodie's paradise, home to hundreds of boulangeries, chocolates, and stylish cafés ideal for weekend brunch and people-watching.

Then take a leisurely walk through the lovely grounds of the Musée de la Vie Romantique, one of the few free museums in Paris, and then visit the namesake Pigalle streetwear shop. With a variety of choices for having fun after sundown, So-Pi is especially well known for its nightlife.

In a tiki-themed setting, Dirty Dick is the place to go for rum, while upscale Le Carmen provides drinks in a sumptuous, very Parisian atmosphere. The area's attractions are trendy rather than historically significant. For basketball fans, Pigalle Duperré is a neon-colored court tucked between two enormous apartment buildings.

3. The Marais

The Marais is the place to go if you're seeking this type of Parisian romance. It has well-kept squares, beautiful parks with secret fountains, classic bistros, and little fashion shops. In addition to having a sizable LGBTQ+ population living there, this neighborhood is renowned for housing a variety of independent art galleries and specialty shops tucked amid affluent houses.

The majority of new pubs and clubs may be appearing in Paris' more inexpensive, roomier east, but the Marais will always rank among the city's top neighborhoods for accommodations. Its extravagantly opulent hôtels particuliers and classic boulangeries give off the impression of being a perfect representation of Paris. It is well situated geographically.

On the right side of the Seine, across from Notre Dame, the Marais is dispersed throughout the 3rd and 4th arrondissements. You may locate the Hôtel de Ville, the Louvre, and the Tuileries to your west, and the lively bars of Bastille to your east. The Centre Pompidou is also close by.

The remodeled Musée Picasso and the majestic Place des Vosges are both located in the Marais. When you're starving, go to Breizh Café for delectable galettes and crêpes or the delightfully odd Derrière for contemporary French food served in an opulent apartment.

4. Bastille

Consider Bastille as your base in Paris since it is close to the Marais but far less expensive. To begin with, there are several top-notch places to dine and drink in the region. Try to get a reservation at Septime for elegant meals that won't cost the earth. Bookings only become available every three months and sell out quickly, so beware.

The place to go for coffee and cuddling is Café des Chats in Paris. For those seeking to purchase some French sass, the Rue de Charonne is home to some amazing stores, and Opéra Bastille always offers a great lineup of events, so be sure to check what's on well in advance. Wander along the Coulée Verte's repurposed railroad tracks in the late afternoon for a breath of fresh air.

5. Montmartre

The majority of people's perceptions of Paris are based on Montmartre, which has streets lined with vintage cafés, ivy-covered apartment buildings, and sacré-gleaming colors white domes. So why not let your dreams run wild? Thanks to its steep slopes, adorable multicolored cottages, and little old-world businesses, this northern district has managed to keep its delightful village vibe.

Explore the neighborhood looking for spots from "Amélie," pay a visit to the Cimetière Montmartre to see where Degas and Zola are buried, and enjoy the enchanted rose gardens of the Musée de Montmartre, which dates to the

17th century. Many restaurants are competing for your euros, but avoid the tourist traps by visiting Il Brigante, Soul Kitchen, or Le Coq Rico instead. Visit the Terrass Hotel's rooftop bar, the cozy Bar à Bulles above the Moulin Rouge, or go all out at Le Très Particulier for beverages.

6. Oberkampf

The neighborhood between Bastille and République, where the Rue Oberkampf is lined with several clubs, offers some of Paris's greatest nightlife. Everything from upscale cocktail lounges to gritty wine bars may be found here. You will undoubtedly discover a drinking establishment that suits you in this area of Paris, which has the most active nightlife.

Regardless of the time of day, the area is great for strolling, but after dark, Oberkampf comes alive. Bars like the brilliantly kitsch Ave Maria and beautifully restored Café Charbon are worth visiting before visiting the renowned music venue Le Bataclan for top-notch national and international live acts. Additionally, if all that drinking has you peckish, try the contemporary French tapas at Aux Deux Amis or Ober Mamma's reasonably-priced pasta and pizza.

7. Canal St. Martin

Since a few years ago, this charming, cobbled area of town meandering from République up to Stalingrad has been a must-see location. The bike-friendly Canal Saint-Martin, which has a noticeably slower pace of life than other parts of Paris, has gained popularity among foodies for its abundance of organic wine and cheese shops, specialty coffee shops, and restaurants offering cuisine with an international influence.

This is the area for you if you like eating. The neighboring Parc des Buttes-Chaumont, however, with its waterfalls, grottoes, and Italian-style Temple de la Sybille, is a terrific spot to go for a walk and burn off some of those calories. If you want to go farther, you may hire a Vélib bike and ride up to La Villette. You must go to Ten Belles, Bob's Bake Shop, Chez Prune, Centre Commercial, and Holybelly.

8. Belleville

After spending the day seeing some of Paris' more upscale districts, the bustle of Chinatown with its graffiti-covered alleyways and cramped canteens might be a bit of a shock. But there are issues in this area. Before treating yourself to top-notch Chinese cuisine on the Rue de Belleville, browse the area's many independent restaurants and pubs and enjoy the village-like atmosphere.

The greatest grilled dumplings in Paris can be found at Ravioli Chinois Nord-Est (two minute walk from the popular Belleville metro intersection), which also serves huge sharing dishes ideal for parties. La Bellevilloise, an all-day playground, and Le Lapin Blanc, a wine bar, are located close to Ménilmontant in the southern region. The legendary celebrity cemetery Père-Lachaise is nearby, as are the Buttes-Chaumont and the Canal Saint-banks. Martin's

9. Les Champs-Élysées.

The glitzy neighborhood around the Champs-Elysées may not be your first choice when choosing a hotel location. It is most strongly linked with the Grand Palais, Arc de Triomphe, and oh yes, France's most renowned shopping boulevard. However, this affluent area is a fantastic starting point for exploring the city on foot or by bicycle. The Musée Galliera, Palais de Tokyo, and Petit Palais are just a few of the many attractions close for art lovers.

For those with a sweet craving, late-opening Pierre Hermé and Ladurée locations can be found at the Marché Président Wilson, a must-visit market that is stocked with fresh flowers and organic products. One of Paris's smaller, more attractive parks, Parc Monceau, is located north of the 8th arrondissement and is dotted with sculptures and neoclassical follies.

Take a trip in the Bateaux-Mouches to view Paris from the river, or stroll along the Seine's banks and stop at one of the numerous pop-up bars. Except Le Drugstore, avoid the tourist traps on the Champs-Elysees and go down a side street for a genuine flavor of Paris at its poshest.

Cost Of Food In Paris

Planning a trip budget may be challenging, particularly in a city with so many possibilities.
In Paris, there is no limit on how much you may spend, thus practicing self-control can sometimes be difficult. But having a nice time or enjoying dinner doesn't have to be expensive!

We've broken down what some of your expenses would be at each meal so you can estimate the typical cost of food in Paris each day. How well you can dine even on a tight budget may surprise you, in our opinion!

Breakfast

Don't worry if it isn't offered by your hotel. The lightest meal of the day is breakfast in France, where you can get a handcrafted croissant for around one euro at any of the city's many boulangeries. Furthermore, there is no need to be concerned about wasting valuable touring time. Breakfast pastries are often consumed on the move or on a public bench rather than at a café or restaurant, where they might cost up to three times as much.

If you want a café crème on the outside terrace (coffee with milk is seldom referred to as a café au lait by locals), coffee may be a bit more pricey. There are often three separate drink pricing in pubs and restaurants where you pay for your real estate. Sipping an espresso while standing at the bar will often just cost you €1, yet sitting inside will cost you €2, and sitting outdoors can sometimes cost you more than €2.50 for the same cup of coffee.

Lunch

It's wise to dine at home or get takeout at least once a day if you're on a limited budget. Avoid having it as lunch once!

The formula, a fixed-price meal with one, two, or three dishes, can be found during lunchtime in Paris and is one of the greatest bargains in the city. The formula, which is only available between 12 p.m. and 3 p.m., is often written on a blackboard, is updated every day, and is priced at less than €25 for three dishes. Simply ordering the plat du jour, or meal of the day will run you around €15.

Dinner

Most restaurants only provide a less-priced plat du jour during lunch, making dinner potentially more expensive. Without a drink, the price of a main dish will start at roughly €20.

Dinner is the ideal time to sample some of Paris' greatest street cuisine if you're on a tight budget. As an alternative, get a baguette, some cheese, and a bottle of wine and go down to the Seine to join the locals who are having a lovely picnic there.

Drinks

You got it: wine is the most affordable alcoholic beverage in France. If you're on a tight budget, you can get a bottle in the grocery store for around €3, and if not, there's no upper limit!

A bottle of wine typically costs between €20 and €25 in bars and restaurants. Beer is pricey—it costs around €7 for a pint—but from 6 to 8 p.m., happy hours are offered all across the city. The cost of local spirits prevents them from being often consumed. Cocktail prices often begin at about $12.

One of our favorite urban Paris wineries is Les Vignerons Parisiens.
For good reason, France is regarded as one of the world's top wine-producing regions.

What is the average daily cost of food in Paris?

We estimate that it will cost around €50 per person per day to eat your way through Paris. Even though you may save even more money by going on a picnic and solely consuming street food, we believe it's good to spend part of your hard-earned money on dining out in the city that pioneered the restaurant!

Top Paris Attractions To See And Explore

For many tourists, these are the top attractions in Paris since they are the historical, cultural, and well-known locations that everyone associates with the city.

Don't feel as if you have to see each one at a single visit, particularly if you are only staying a short while. Various of them are visible from many locations across the city, whether or not you are there, including the majestic Arc de Triomphe, the majestic Seine River, the towering

Eiffel Tower, and even the sparkling white Sacre Coeur perched high on a hilltop.

The Latin Quarter and Montmartre are two examples of famous neighborhoods that are worth seeing. Enjoy the lovely Luxembourg Garden and unwind. Embark on a Seine sunset cruise.

Admire the Notre Dame Cathedral for a while. Sadly, because of the terrible fire in 2019, you can only see the outside. However, if restoration work is completed as planned by 2024, at least a tiny portion of the majestic cathedral could be accessible to the public. The exquisite South and North Rose Windows, which date to the 13th century, are only one of the irreplaceable gems of the cathedral that avoided major harm. Someday, you'll get another chance to see them.

And schedule a trip to at least one of Paris' most renowned museums to see the amazing artwork there. View the Venus of Milo and the Mona Lisa at the Louvre, Starry Night by Van Gogh at the Orsay, or cutting-edge contemporary art at the Pompidou.

Last but not least, allot some time even if it means missing some of the locations on this list to explore some less well-known and even "secret" sights in Paris. You may always stop by when you return to Paris, and in the meanwhile, you'll have plenty of beautiful memories.

Since Paris is a mobile feast, as Ernest Hemingway famously observed, "... wherever you go for the rest of your life it remains with you."

1. Eiffel Tower (Tour Eiffel)

The Eiffel Tower, which rises majestically over the Parisian countryside and offers breathtaking city views from three levels, is a symbol of Paris. Going to the top of the Eiffel Tower is often listed as one of the best things to do in Paris, France, and with good reason.

Although you can view the iconic monument from numerous locations across the city, nothing compares to the excitement of climbing up to the observation decks and seeing the Paris landmarks below you becoming smaller and smaller.

By scheduling a professional picture session in front of the famous structure, you may immortalize the memories of your trip for all time.

Interested in just seeing this well-known Parisian landmark? A Seine River cruise is the ideal way to visit it, as well as the many other renowned sites and museums situated along the river.

There is also a champagne bar, restaurants, a first-floor transparent floor with amazing views, and an ice rink that is open seasonally during certain years.

Paris Discovery Tip: If you prepare ahead, you may skip the standard queue at the Eiffel Tower despite the large crowds and long lines for tickets that can last up to 4 hours or more during peak months.

2. Louvre Museum (Musée du Louvre)

The enormous Louvre Museum receives over 10 million visitors a year, making it the world's most visited museum and a top attraction in the part of the 1st arrondissement known as "Royal Paris."

The Mona Lisa by Leonardo da Vinci and two well-known Greek statues the Venus de Milo and the Winged Victory of Samothrace which served as the model for the well-known sports shoe company, Winged Nike are largely responsible for its popularity.

But the Louvre gives you so much more to view, such as a great Egyptian collection replete with mummies, gallery after gallery of European paintings from the Middle Ages to the mid-19th century, and stunning rooms of superb furniture, tapestries, and decorative things.

Outside, a reflecting pool and glass pyramids by I M Pei from the 20th century stand in contrast to the previous royal palace's elaborate Renaissance architecture.

More to Enjoy: You can see the excavations of the ancient castle from the 12th century that formerly stood where the Louvre is now in Paris down in the basement.

Paris Discovery Tip: Due to a large number of visitors, you'll need the plan to make the most of your time at this museum. But don't worry, you have several great alternatives, from priority tickets that must be purchased in advance to guided tours.

3. Versailles Palace

One of the biggest palaces in the world, Versailles Palace has more than 700 rooms.

Versailles Palace offers a unique look into royal life when you visit. It is renowned for its royal occupants, including King Louis XIV and Marie-Antoinette, and is home to the shimmering Hall of Mirrors, opulently adorned chambers, and valuable paintings. Here, you might easily spend most or the whole day.

Additional attractions include magnificent gardens with strolling routes, fountains, sculptures, and flowers.

Versailles draws a lot of people, and lengthy security check lines before you can enter necessitate a 2-4 hour wait in line during most months of the year. Paris Discovery Tip: You still need to go through security, even though such lines often move fast. Skip-the-line tickets and attraction passes won't prevent every wait.

4. Latin Quarter (Quartier Latin)

Spend some time exploring the Latin Quarter's attractions to get a feel for older Paris.

This renowned Left Bank area has long drawn bohemians, academics, and political protests. It was first populated by Romans in the first century. The ancient, twisting lanes and buildings may be used as reminders of medieval Paris if you look attentively.

Visit the Pantheon to see the graves of French philosophers and heroes, have a drink at a brasserie along Boulevard Saint Germain, and admire the Lady and the Unicorn tapestries at the Cluny Museum for their eternal beauty.

Explore the quaint, meandering side lanes that are home to vintage bookshops, quaint restaurants, and eccentric shops for additional enjoyment. Visit the stunning, historic cathedrals packed with works of art, including Saint Julien le Pauvre, who lived throughout the Middle Ages. One of the Latin Quarter's "secret jewels" will take you even farther back in time: a Roman arena from the first century.

Avoid the pedestrian-only Rue de la Huchette unless you like crowded areas.

5. Seine River - Beaches, Cruises, & More

Central Paris is divided between the Right Bank to the north and the Left Bank to the south by the Seine River. The historic center of Paris is located on Île de la Cité, one of two little islands in the middle, and it is home to renowned medieval masterpieces, secret gardens, and charming 17th-century neighborhoods.

There are several ways to appreciate the Seine. Admire the lovely bridges while strolling along the banks. Les bouquinistes, the Seine's riverside bookshops, are worth seeing. Discover the Parc Rives de Seine, a pedestrian-only riverbank walkway that runs from the Place de la Bastille to the Eiffel Tower.

The most stunning old buildings and bridges in Paris can be seen from a different angle as you go up and down the river on a tour boat. Dine and dance aboard a boat beside the river. Cool off in a swimming pool that is floating.

Visit Les Berges, the riverside leisure area on the Left Bank; the summer is when it comes to life.

The Right Bank and other areas of the city are turned into a sandy beach by Paris Plages from mid-July until mid-August.

Paris Travel Tip: From the Seine, take a boat up along the 15th-century Canal Saint-Martin and Canal de l'Ourcq, passing through the city's increasingly fashionable northeast.

6. Montmartre and Sacré Coeur

Although Montmartre, formerly a distinct town, has been a part of Paris since 1860, its meandering streets, dense tree cover, and gorgeous slopes give the impression that it still exists in a different world.

Imagine the artists, musicians, and authors who called the area home more than a century ago when rentals were affordable as you wander through the neighborhood's many cafés and cabarets.

Most places in Paris may see the sparkling white Basilica of the Sacré Coeur, which was constructed in an Italian Byzantine style.

Tourists often congregate in the regions around Pigalle's Sacré Coeur and the Moulin Rouge theater, but they ignore the most fascinating aspects of the district, which include a few historic windmills, tiny art museums, and parks.

Extras to Enjoy: To see the stunning mosaics, enter Sacré Coeur.

Paris Travel Tip: Attend the harvest festival held in the vineyard that is still in operation at Montmartre if you are in the city in October.

7. Musée d'Orsay

The impressive collection of Impressionist and Post-Impressionist works of art at the Musée d'Orsay, housed in a former railway station, is known across the globe.

The most popular masterpieces are on display in crowded galleries, including those by Monet, Renoir, Cézanne, Gauguin, and Van Gogh, whose painting Starry Night draws the biggest crowds of them.

From the almost hidden rooftop patio, you can enjoy breathtaking views of Paris.

Paris Travel Tip: If you want to see the most renowned artworks without being surrounded by throngs of people, take a guided tour, unless you are going during the dull winter months.

8. Arc de Triomphe

Napoleon ordered the enormous Arc de Triomphe in 1806 to commemorate his army's conquests across Europe, but he was exiled and dead by the time it was finished 30 years later, making it one of the most famous Paris sights.

Twelve important streets, including the western end of the Champs Élysées, converge around the Arc de Triomphe in a congested traffic roundabout. While it is visible from a distance, getting near it will provide you with the finest views and experiences.

The first Sunday of each month, often known as "car-free Sundays," when automobiles are prohibited and only pedestrians are allowed, is the best day to see.

Get a ticket and ascend the steps to the observation deck at the top for a 360-degree panorama of Paris for more enjoyment. Visit the everlasting flame and Tomb of the Unknown

Soldier at the foot of the monument to pay respects to the unnamed French soldiers who died in World Wars I and II. Every evening at 6:30 pm, you may see it being re-lit. Large areas of the monument are covered with elaborate statuary and bas-relief carvings that depict the campaigns of Napoleon.

Paris Discovery Tip: If you're in Paris on Armistice Day (November 11), Bastille Day (July 14), or New Year's Eve (December 31), don't miss the parades and festivities on the Champs Élysées that begin at the Arc. The Paris Marathon in April also starts and ends there, and the Tour de France also concludes there in July.

9. Pompidou Center (Centre Pompidou)

When the Pompidou Center initially opened, there were shouts of mockery at its avant-garde design, which featured outside walls of vividly colored tubes and exposed mechanical systems in a city full of conventional buildings. Renzo Piano and Richard Rogers' architectural vision for the structure is still distinctive in the cityscape more than fifty years later.

But inside, changing exhibits of outstanding modern paintings, sculptures, and video and sound works are what makes the museum so well-liked (buy a skip-the-line ticket before you arrive to save time).

More to enjoy: A lovely rooftop terrace, a reflecting pool, and a restaurant with city views.

The Stravinsky Fountain, which bears the composer's name and is filled with 16 water-spraying moving sculptures that depict his music, can be found behind the Centre Pompidou on the right side. If you gaze directly down from the rooftop deck, you can also see it.

10. Luxembourg Garden (Jardin du Luxembourg)

Luxembourg Garden is Paris's most well-liked park thanks to its towering chestnut trees, a serene lagoon where kids (and adolescents and adults) float toy sailboats and several chairs for people-watching among the park's luxuriant foliage and magnificent monuments.

With 448 more municipal parks and 2 magnificent kinds of wood to select from, that difference is significant.

Luxembourg Garden has a large number of visitors, yet it never seems crowded since it is separated into several diverse regions throughout its 60 acres. Even tennis is available here.

There's more to enjoy, like a meal or a drink at the outside café.

If you're visiting Paris with youngsters, check out the puppet theater and pony rides. If not, grab one of the green metal seats adjacent to the reflecting pool at the Medici Fountain and unwind for a few serene minutes.

More Top Paris Attractions to See & Explore

Rodin Museum (Musée Rodin)

Perhaps the most romantic museum in Paris and a top attraction because of its lush sculpture garden, location in a spectacular 18th century rococo mansion, and, of course, the sensual sculpture of two lovers in "The Kiss, the Rodin Museum gives you the opportunity to view the breadth and depth of French sculptor Auguste Rodin's boundary-breaking path from naturalism to modernism.

Plan to spend more time than you might expect in the beautifully designed garden, where flowers bloom almost year-round, lime trees scent the air with their leaves, and masses of roses burst into a riot of color in May and June, with some continuing to bloom through fall.

The garden is also where you'll see Rodin's most monumental and evocative creations: "The

Thinker," "Walking Man," "The Gates of Hell," to name only a few.

Monet's Garden at Giverny & Other Day Trips from Paris

Other top sights you can visit on day trips from Paris include the Palace of Versailles, Monet's well-known water lily ponds and garden at Giverny, the medieval abbey at Mont Saint-Michel, Disneyland Paris, the Normandy D-Day beaches, exclusive Champagne-tasting tours, and stunning castles and chateaux.

Even if you depart from Paris in the morning, you can spend the day taking in the sights in London, enjoying delectable food and wine at a château surrounded by vineyards near Bordeaux, or cruising through the charming canals of Bruges, Belgium, and still make it back to Paris in time for a late dinner.

Paris Food Tours, Wine Tastings, & More Culinary Adventures

Want to explore Paris's culinary culture, which is unquestionably one of the city's most well-known attractions, while also discovering a famous neighborhood, sailing the Seine River, making macarons, going to a street market, or tasting wine and cheese?

In addition to one of Paris's booming craft breweries, we showcase 15 of the greatest food and wine-related excursions, cruises, and workshops.

The Paris Skyline

One of the city's most recognizable sights is the Paris skyline, which is made up of iconic buildings like the Eiffel Tower, Sacre Coeur, and Notre Dame silhouetted against the sky and city roofs. What are the greatest locations to see it, though?

Some of them, like the observation decks on the Eiffel Tower and the rooftop terrace of the Arc de Triomphe, are expected. Others, though, fall firmly into the "insider secret" category and are hidden spots where you can see the Paris skyline and may not find them on your own..

Père Lachaise Cemetery

Even while the Père Lachaise Cemetery (Cimetière du Père Lachaise) in eastern Paris isn't as as well-known as the Eiffel Tower or the Arc de Triomphe, its famed tombs, eerie monuments, and picturesque cobblestone alleys make it a must-see destination in Paris.

This "City of the Dead" is both a cemetery and a beautifully landscaped garden, with funerary sculptures of every size and shape imaginable, including chubby winged cherubs, macabre skulls flanked by what appear to be bat wings, scantily clad women sprawled across tombstones, and disembodied heads of famous men. It also resembles an outdoor museum.

The graves of notable individuals interred here, though, could pique your interest the most if you're like the majority of first-time visitors.

CHAPTER 4

Basic French Phrases

- Bonjour - Hello
- Merci - Thank you
- S'il vous plaît - Please
- Excusez-moi - Excuse me
- Oui - Yes
- Non - No
- Je ne comprends pas - I don't understand
- Parlez-vous anglais? - Do you speak English?
- Où est ...? - Where is ...?
- Combien ça coûte? - How much does it cost?
- Je voudrais ... - I would like ...
- Je cherche ... - I'm looking for ...
- C'est combien? - How much is it?
- Je m'appelle ... - My name is ...
- Au revoir - Goodbye

When visiting another country, it's usually a good idea to learn a few fundamental words since it shows respect for the local way of life and may facilitate conversation. Additionally, knowing these French expressions will be helpful while requesting directions, placing an order for food, or even striking up a basic chat with Parisians.

Staying Safe In Paris

These suggestions can help you explore Paris calmly.
Here are some fundamental rules and sensible mindsets to embrace to truly appreciate Paris:

1. Be vigilant for pickpockets

Pickpockets are drawn to crowded settings, especially tourist regions. Therefore, it's crucial to exercise caution, keep your stuff in your bag, make sure it's securely fastened, and carry it in front of you at all times.

2. Make payments with a bank card.

Avoid carrying a lot of cash to prevent theft (and if you have some, keep your eye on it). Favor payments are made via a bank card or a mobile device.

3. Remain watchful

Keep an eye out for any strange activity, such as someone approaching you and requesting that you sign (false) petitions or participate in a scam called "bonneteau" (a game using three cards or three plastic cups). These are methods for keeping you from paying attention to your personal property.

4. Always keep your luggage nearby.

Keep your luggage and any personal stuff close at hand.

5. Keep a copy of your ID documents.

Even in their digital form in your email box, make copies of your identification documents and save them safely. You will always have a backup copy of these important papers in case of loss or theft.

6. After your ID documents are stolen or lost, contact the appropriate authorities.

Contact your consulate and report the incident to the police if your identification documents are lost or stolen. These authorities will support you in carrying out the required administrative procedures.

7. Contact an emergency line if you are attacked.

Make as much noise as you can to attract the attention of anybody around and seek shelter someplace secure if you are being attacked. Call

17 to reach the police or 112 to reach the emergency services.

8. Contact SAVE to file a complaint in any language.

A software program called the help system for foreign victims enables any foreigner to file a complaint in their language with a police officer. To streamline administrative processes at their embassy, the police officer will then provide them with a receipt in their native tongue.

Food To Eat In Paris And Where To Try Them

While in the French city, you may climb the Eiffel Tower, walk down the Champs-Elysées, and then spend the remainder of your time getting lost in the Louvre's collection of artwork. However, you would completely lose out if you don't eat out while in Paris.

French culture is deeply rooted in its cuisine. In 2010, UNESCO recognized the French manner of eating as an Intangible Cultural Heritage.

There is only one way to comprehend the nation's passion for our cuisine: consume it all! Or at the very least, begin with some of Paris' most well-known cuisine.

The best approach to falling in love with French cuisine is with these seven samples of well-known meals from Paris. We've even included a suggested place or two where you might test each to make your task simpler. Good appetite!

1. Croissants: inexpensive yet indelible

Get yourself an all-butter croissant for breakfast to start your day off right like a real Parisian!

Croissants may look simple, but these perfectly flaky pastries require time (we're talking several days!) and a whole set of skills to perfect.

Whether you have them with your coffee, orange juice, or on their own, croissants are guaranteed to brighten up your morning!

Additionally, there's no need to stress about wasting valuable tourist time by sitting down for breakfast. Breakfast on the go is very fine here in France, so you may have your croissant anywhere. Lunch and supper are more revered sit-down activities.

Where to find them: Only order pastries from real artisan bakeries, and avoid frozen factory croissants. La Maison d'Isabelle (47 ter Boulevard Saint-Germain) is a fantastic choice and just won the prize for Best Croissant in Paris. The boulangerie uses certified Charente-Poitou butter and organic flour to create unique croissants.

2. Escargots: A emblem of the country
You really must taste these before leaving Paris!

Although there are several methods to prepare snails in Paris, the Burgundy dish is still the most common. The escargots, which are often served in groups of twelve, are served in their shells and packed with a delectable mixture of garlic, herbs, and butter.

But since they are now so well-liked, escargots have inspired other Parisian eateries to reinvent the dish. Snails are currently offered in a variety of sauces, including curry-based, truffle, and Roquefort.

What's the greatest part, you ask? Escargots are not only tasty, but they are also a great source of iron and magnesium.

When trying them: A genuine Parisian institution, L'Escargot Montorgueil has been serving snails for over 200 years. You may taste the classic Burgundy or switch it up with the curry, foie gras, or truffle butter varieties!

3. Macarons

The finest thing that could have ever happened to French confections, macarons are not to be confused with macaroons, which are treats made with crushed coconut. Their light and airy almond flour shells are filled with a creamy, decadent filling.

Nobody is absolutely clear where these famous snacks originate from. Some accounts attribute the concept to Catherine de Medici, while others attribute it to a French Carmelite monastery from the late 18th century. Regardless of whose version of the legend you accept, macarons may very well be the most well-known dish served in Paris at the moment.

Pistachio, chocolate, vanilla, and raspberry are popular tastes, but don't be afraid to experiment with some of the more odd flavors, such as salted butter caramel, green tea, or rose petals, to mention a few.

When trying them: There are several macaron-specific stores in Paris, and the majority of them provide amazing quality. For his creativity—and his Balinese dark chocolate macaron—Pierre Hermé continues to be one of our obvious favorites.

Dessert enthusiasts might also try Sadaharu Aoki's "Symphony," a creative dish from his hometown of Tokyo. His delicious violet macaron is stuffed with fresh raspberries, violet, and earl gray cream. Délicieux!

4. Jambon-beurre: The greatest in Parisian street cuisine

Who knew that sandwiches could be so delicious?

The secret to this popular lunchtime snack is simplicity. The quality of the jambon-three beurre's simple ingredients—Parisian ham, butter, and, of course, the delectably crispy baguette—is what makes it so outstanding.

However, since there are so few ingredients, it is important to make sure that each one is of the highest quality. That entails a baguette with the ideal amount of crust, superb French butter, and authentic Parisian ham. (Yes, there is a difference between this and regular ham.)

Where to test it out: The jambon-beurre sandwich at La Fontaine de Belleville, which is made with carefully chosen ingredients, is well-known across the city. You may choose to take it to go or eat it outside on the patio with a green salad.

5. Tartare de steak

Although not everyone likes eating raw meat, those who do so will be rewarded with very delectable cuisine.

A bistro staple, steak tartare is made of raw ground beef that has been seasoned with capers, onion, and black pepper. It is often served with an egg yolk that is still raw on top.

Despite being widely consumed in France today, steak tartare originated in Mongolia. Russian sailors introduced it to Europe in the 17th century, and the rest is history.

Where to try it: Le Severo is a carnivore's paradise, therefore the meat will be of the highest caliber possible. They serve their insanely delicious steak tartare with either french fries or green beans.

6. Cheddar

Former French president Charles De Gaulle famously said, "How can you rule a nation when there are 246 types of cheese?" We don't know the answer, but we do know that going to such a place will be fun!

In reality, France has over 300 different kinds of cheese, from the creamy Brie de Meaux to the sour Munster. There are now more than 300 reasons to appreciate French cheese!

In modern France, cheese is esteemed so highly that it has earned a position in the meal. Traditionally, a cheese course is placed between the entrée and the dessert (or sometimes in place of the latter).

A La Ville de Rodez, located at 22 Rue Vieille du Temple, has been a cheese lover's paradise since 1920.

7. Tomato soup

Onion soup is among the most reassuring foods and another popular dish in Paris.

The recipe is said to have been created by Louis XV close to three centuries ago. A piece of Gruyère cheese is now placed on top of the gratinéed caramelized onion and beef broth dish. And, of course, it tastes just as amazing as it does.

Traditional French onion soup is as easy to make as they come, which speaks to how seriously we in France take our cuisine. Where else on earth could the modest onion be brought to such gastronomic heights?

Where to try it: Order it at the wonderful Bistrot des Vosges, where the handmade, to-die-for onion soup is created.

CHAPTER 5

Suggested Budget

Taking into account the costs of other tourists, you should budget around €184 ($200) each day for your Paris holiday. In the past, tourists have typically spent €31 ($34) on meals for a day and €17 ($18) on local transportation. Additionally, a couple may book a hotel in Paris for an average of €242 ($263). Therefore, a vacation to Paris for two individuals for a week typically costs €2,572 ($2,797). To assist you in creating your trip budget, we have compiled all of these typical travel costs from other travelers.

Typically, a weeklong holiday in Paris runs around €1,286 for one person. So, for two individuals, a weeklong vacation to Paris will cost around €2,572. In Paris, a two-week holiday for two individuals would set you back €5,144. Since children's tickets are less expensive and hotel rooms may be shared, the cost of a trip for a family of three or four usually decreases. Your daily budget will decrease as you move more slowly and for a longer amount of time. A two-person trip to Paris for a month may often cost less per person per day than a one-person trip to Paris for a week.

24-hours Itinerary

1 Day in Paris

8:00 AM - Start the day with a classic French breakfast of croissants and coffee at a local café.

9:00 AM - Visit Notre-Dame Cathedral, a masterpiece of Gothic architecture.

10:30 AM - Walk along the Seine River to the Île de la Cité, the birthplace of Paris.

11:00 AM - Explore the Sainte-Chapelle, a 13th-century church with stunning stained-glass windows.

12:00 PM - Have lunch at a traditional French bistro in the Latin Quarter.

1:30 PM - Visit the famous Louvre Museum, home to the Mona Lisa and thousands of other masterpieces.

4:00 PM - Take a stroll through the Luxembourg Gardens, a beautiful park in the heart of the city.

5:00 PM - Visit the famous Eiffel Tower, one of the most iconic landmarks in Paris. Take the stairs or elevator to the top for panoramic views of the city.

7:00 PM - Enjoy a romantic dinner at a charming Parisian restaurant.

9:00 PM - Take a night-time boat tour along the Seine River to admire the illuminated city landmarks.

10:30 PM - End the night with a glass of Champagne at a jazz club or cabaret show.

This itinerary offers a perfect blend of historical and cultural experiences, with some time to relax and enjoy the city's charming atmosphere. It can be adjusted based on personal preferences and time availability.

CONCLUSION

Finally, Paris is a place that genuinely captures the spirit of art, culture, and history. Every tourist may find something to enjoy in Paris, from its stunning architecture to its famous museums and delectable cuisine. If you're looking for a romantic holiday, a unique cultural experience, or just a taste of the high life, this city is guaranteed to make an impact. There is always plenty to see and do in Paris, whether it is enjoying a café au lait at a sidewalk café, wandering along the Seine River's banks, or admiring master painters' creations at the Louvre Museum.

However, Paris is much more than its famous buildings and popular tourist destinations. A strong feeling of community, a thriving culture, and a long history all characterize this city. A contagious love for life can be found here together with a special fusion of contemporary elegance and old-world charm. Paris is a city that just brims with vitality, from its throbbing street markets and inviting sidewalk cafés to its lovely parks and recognizable buildings.

Paris is a place that guarantees to amaze you whether you are a seasoned tourist or a first-time visitor. Pack your luggage, grab your camera, and get ready for a once-in-a-lifetime trip to one of the most enchanting cities on earth. Greetings from your destination!

Printed in Great Britain
by Amazon